PLAYERS

PLAYERS

John Nyman

819.16
NYMAN

Palimpsest Press
1171 Eastlawn Ave.
Windsor, Ontario. N8s 3J1
www.palimpsestpress.ca

Book and cover design by Dawn Kresan. Typeset in Adobe Garamond Pro and Krungthep, and printed offset on Zephyr Laid at Coach House Printing in Ontario, Canada. Edited by Jim Johnstone.

Palimpsest Press would like to thank the Canada Council for the Arts, and the Ontario Arts Council for their support of our publishing program. We also acknowledge the assistance of the Government of Ontario through the Ontario Book Publishing Tax Credit.

Canada Council for the Arts	Conseil des Arts du Canada	ONTARIO ARTS COUNCIL CONSEIL DES ARTS DE L'ONTARIO	Ontario Ontario Media Development Corporation

Library and Archives Canada Cataloguing in Publication

Nyman, John, author
        Players / John Nyman.

Poems.
ISBN 978-1-926794-30-3 (paperback)

        I. Title.

PS8627.Y52P53 2016   C811'.6   C2016-900152-0

for my sisters
and my parents

Two False Starts

The Losers

Fast Breaks

Two False Starts

The Mole Rat

Maybe a poem for the cool of the bus
in my hair,
like the whole network
of hidden bloodlines
in clear eyes, or the air
rattling under the stop-caller's
words.

When a container empties
completely,
even slightness
engorges it, fills out
its corners again,
a deep network
of trust, tensile thin.

The mole rat
tunnelling in the black dirt
works towards brightness blind,
hands careening and ears blowing up
at every new depth.

Understandable

Speaking of elegance, let me justify myself.
We are the products of everything around us.
All the colours go together.

First, there is a pattern,
then there is another pattern,
and their relation is a pattern in itself.

When I look into your eyes, I like what I see
in what you see, but the shadow blows by.
And isn't it just so?

I want to make it different from the recent trend
that all kinds of people who used to be cool
are falling, falling, falling, falling into.

I was on the cusp of something more,

believe it. This isn't meant as a stab against anyone,
but I do fly higher.
And that's why we're here today.

The Losers

To KiD CuDi

I'll tell you what I know about dreaming:
it's blue, a sad blue, and it spotlights
my ribs where your hook jacks me—rounded
like a cane—and drops me, empty, offstage,

coughing. Tell me what you know about night.
The way it pulls the terrors from daylight
like a bong hit, that smooth calamity,
crisp fatness. The hurt that comes with cool,

and without cool. Then, explain: how do you
fall unconscious every night?
Picture, for me, the world's most sweet extremes.
Tell me, what do you know about dreaming?

—that blue self I just want to be golden,
that soul I hope remains, like yours—like
anyone's—unnamed.

Edward Hopper, *Nighthawks*

All this waiting, let's make it a game, then.
Hello to myself and to you, 3 friends,
let's claim which of us

is the uniformed duplicate, back to the camera.
Which is the white-hearted servant,
the guy, the red doll.

Too bad it only works if you're all 4 in a hole.
Or if you're me, my mom, and my 2 sisters
at my grandmother's lover's funeral.

You'd think anyone could reach down, pull out a treat. No:
anyone can, phosphorescent, match a face.
Anyone can turn their back.

At least the street won't change, much.
This isn't much of a game—
just elongates everything.

vita longissima est.

I spend a long time cutting my fingernails,
admiring, pursing my lips and blowing.

I spend a long time
on the toilet,

a long time
asleep.

Long times
parsed by sighing, rows of dashes
yawning.

Remember,
there is a lot of waiting.

How to Hustle

I'll sell ice in the winter, I'll sell fire in Hell,
I am a hustler, baby, I'll sell water to a well.
—Jay Z

Stones:

remain stony; harden
    to any intent;
uphold all footings ardently,
unrelenting, until
    the point you're spent;
texture yourself according
    to what's outside.

Signals:

externalize; moult
    readily, emerge;
always flee, but never fear
to surge into the slipstream
    of erasure;
Hello! you'll say, *my name is*
    whatever's coming.

Vehicles:

love running; cross
    anything static;
clear those currents routed
against traffic, and appear
    as fast as magic;
force any space to fold
    to any motion.

Investments:

hold on; persist
    as liquid until pressed;
decide the value everything
expresses, with nothing extra
    except interest;
you're weightless—equivalent,
    in process, not quite done.

Plants:

require sun; wither
    at bad fortune;
be lightly directed, blind-sighted
by absorption; may your roots
    never shorten;
merely breathe and eat
    within the bubble.

Hustlers:

keep hustling; make
    your marks enthralled;
come through with the utilities
called for, but when you move,
    be barely resolved;
add only a little more.
    Just a little more.

Bouquet

The pink plastic rose. The inner folds of real flowers or very good replicas. Filtered water. The visual texture of marble.

Couch cushions. Brick. Cotton sleep. The screen door held open by the wind. The parakeet in the background. A sliver. Bits of glass. A dandelion. Figures in the communal garden. Hydro towers. Reservoir. Complaining about complaining about the heat. Dandelions.

Two empty benches, one nearer to us and one at which we will sit. Quatrains. Blonde. A substantial coin. A glowing arrow, pointing left, in the night, when it became cool. All of it throwaway. *In my dream… I don't remember.* Corrugation. Metal. Sharing. Sweat, and sleep.

Without failing, a surrender. A flash of our old dog, or just a picture. A yellow car. A grey car, a gash across the side door. Rock candy in small jars with label glue still on. Apricots. The library at sunset. Neon lime. Space tomatoes. Annual, biennial and perennial.

Drunken Master

I wish there was another way to explain
how every good fight is like a dream, a dream
you dream on your enemy's floor
once he's bested, and the floor
sweet-sick and sweat-damp
as a bed.

Also, how arguing with father at the railway
was like drinking, then sleeping off the night
and waking to the memory like you'd just had it.

So why'd I lie a lie like *I won't ever
drink again?* Or lie at all?
Especially that deadpan tract
that Peace will win. I mean, to say some men
won't leap through windows, spears drawn, after you,
and other men won't have to fight them back,
rending them together like flesh, like
of a feather, and the colour into which
they all melted—
joyous, sure.
And beheaded.

But then, they aren't so unlike us
fast sticking friends, clung
like blades attacking in the house of love,
slashes sharp as a crush.

And how this swell, intoxicated boxer hangs back,
surrenders himself to anything,

bewildered.

Nosferatu

Like a regular man bound tight,
or a ghost stretched thin
at the outskirts,
its instincts are stealth and madness;
this is its work.
It rips at your heart
and spirit, your consciousness.
If it rips at your skin
it's invisible, leaves little,
twin canine pips and
you think nothing of it.

If you remember a monster, it is infestation,
ruining life from inside—
the smell of rat-holes in your drywall,
sound of a cockroach
on the kitchen table
before you snap the lights on
at night, most frightening in negation,
most frightening when it is nowhere
to be found.

Myself as a Dictator

External segments are safer,
brutally new as a coin,
so I am regarding facts,
equally firm as plausible,
to parcel upon you, temporary explanation,

veritable, sheer and uprooted,
because information liquidates,
so I apologize simply,
with unadulterated emphasis,
to hint at the obvious, deeper organization,

chiefly inner and driving,
at some instances, freedom,
so I am certainly speaking,
basically reliable horror,
to supply your alliance, psychological resort.

Exit,

a low word, appropriate
for leaving a town
that's awe-slackened all my best friends
into themselves, another old city
swallowing the nostalgia for itself—

a city
     whose cells only felt like a heart's,
     who only reminded me of the ground,

but whose outskirts spritzed
like white pepper, like a simile itch,
a parabola ringing, delimiting,
breathing-in and breathing-out

of Exodus,

a word thrown around
like slang here, in borderlands
that have no right moniker, anyway,
free in their nudity, unnouned—

the sprawl
     that singled me out,
     lifted me up and running

into a body that sticks fast and fucks,
and dies eventually, and rhymes
with the plural of *I*, whose wander rusts
and flits like a good scout.
Here, in this roundabout née

Scarborough,

a word hollow as *exo-*
skeleton, whiff smelled by a hound
who finds she can't hound herself—
land of big roads that roam longer,
skies bright as a pedestrian's aching hunger,
and some ridiculous number
of restaurants, whose strip mall signs' colours
emblazon the infamous banner
of something like an infinite nation—

here I am.

Drunken Master's Apology

I wish I were sober
forever, stuck in stiff
harmony, simple
as a pea-pod separator,
abacus calculator
or hard wooden chair.
I have no inclination
to destruction
when I'm sober. I sit
and think. And if
the wind should blow me,
leaf-like, reality
will replace me. And if another's
hand should snap me,
twig-like, I will simply
break. So, I wish
no wine bottle, beer bottle, sweet liqueur or spirits
pop

Fast Breaks

Future Statement

As the rightward horizon databank overflows
  so spastic backwards engineering has to handle it

splatter the future constellation out the window
  You are in a triangle sideways / Press ENTER

There is bubbly uncorked on the counter / Press ZERO
  A pull of time's arrow twangs blue raspberry

spot-hitting this instant shifting tomorrow
  or pod-perfect homestyle with space-age gingham

rosewater planets percolating intermezzo
  Scanners show we are approaching a black, black object

Naked Baby

Hanlan's Point, Toronto Islands

Round under puff-sun, hot
on the toppling, we're oh-
so seeable, Mama Sol,
sea slurp soapsmooth.
Boom-curves
trump after trump
plus dots and blooms,
shush,
so our sum only dollops
the beachfront dumb
and supples it.

Bouncing buoy-blushing
and sterilized,
I belie
bubbles of wonder…
well, sprung. Lucky
no show's shy
hung in the cosmos
on this *monde bonbon*;
the beach won't even snore
unboldy, its bullion's blues
and straw hues
like a blonde's.

So say we stay plain cute
and naked, balled up
by the sip bumps
doling lull, then tonguing
and snoozing. Swelly,
sunbeams glow an elbow,
navel, pinky—cumulous
as fruit snuck in a bowl
snug through the moons.

TV's Jon Dore on Jon Dore and *The Jon Dore Television Show*

This is the speech I gave at City Hall:
"We need some fucking changes around here,
fuck you all!"
                Three fat cops had to run
across the whole rotunda chasing me,
and when they kicked me out, I kicked the car
parked in the handicap spot. I laughed so hard
I did it twice: for jokes first, then the screen.

Nobody's seen the Jon Dore TV Show,
starring me, TV's Jon Dore. On weekends
I eat noodles from the pot because I'm out
of bowls, and drunk, and poor,
then down them with expired orange juice.
We filmed a shot in my shitty apartment:
we zoomed in on a glass, I dumped
some OJ clunking out of the carton
so bluntly fast it splashed and most of it spilled,
and then we panned and went on with the scene.
Watching it later, in the writers' room,
I laughed and shouted, "Look at that fucktard!
What an awesome cut, and what a moron."

Staring dumbly at my bathroom mirror,
I see a man. A man of iron wit
and meaningful goals?
Never. Maybe, if I were a poet.
But all I see's a shiny pane of glass
with spots of unwashed toothpaste,
mouthwash, shave cream, mucous,
urine, semen, flavoured lube,
and caked on powder cocaine.

…Nobody's laughing.
                    No one's seen the show.

Bibliophile

Skin risks each flipping page, the threat towards
Brain crush. all thinking came from mush, mulch
Virally alive in the grist of pulp. i
Have tics. every end stop i slide a bit;
Every line i survive to drop out
Again. i have red chins and skipping pens
Remind me—no long opening, no wisdom's sin
Can corridor to the world code's end,
Only a bald hollow. i'll yell and i'll yellow,
Type correctly, & recognize
That that too may be risky.
But be this muck, then so be it.

When You Need Water

If the CD skipping in my old-time walkman
sounds like water,
And the me inside is diving out my breastplate hollow to bathe
in the cesspool at the TV,
And his skin is pruny as a thumbprint,
And the blinking light blinks sky blue,
And I'm unpardoned on the wicker sofa,
Well, even the blackboard night might be bigger than my future.
In total, it takes a whole lot of water to breathe.

By the power invested, by the energy skittered away,
Along the rivulet of the second dimension
of the bare-ass moon,
After the water ransacked the follows,
altercations,
Darling, you cross at my side until the changing of the water,
Though I've never really been there in the moment,
And it has never been explained clearly.
Hold it a bullet.

If the smoke is on the water,
If the smoke is beautiful, and by that I mean,
If the last of the pack tastes a lot like an ice cream sundae
just in time…
You've caught me right in the middle of something,
'Cause I'm a stone-cold shame just a-lookin' for some fame,
Or a pointy-haired boss bogarting the water cooler.
Or noodling over a secret,
In a hole in a log at the bottom
of the harshest part of the Outback.

Runtime

A. 999 uses for a thumb tack
off the wall, mind,
two turtle doves and a partridge sailing
the open sea.
1493 is the year of the dog.
One use for silly putty, and I
followed you all the way to this God-forsaken
window to the window to the wall.
A chromosome and—20 minutes later—
my oh my that's another one gone.

B. Discovered in the heat of the furnace,
the right way to look at things
as they may never be again.
That is, better
than the rest, now try to Wake Up!
tired, dead tired
of always being the last one to hear about
hot hot prices.
If you can dance, question: who's the Lincoln?
Answer in the form of the afterlife.
No biggie went to town. Get down.

X. Magic icicle
don't give a damn or a chuckle.
Octopus's eye.

Recorded Instructions for a Secret Agent

    Saunter, sidestep, never tell,
just listen—
    stay cool, fool
them, sing softly
to them.

Point is, this
is the state
of what's missing.
Read on here to the wanting
piece, the counter-turbulent
species of ease,
capital-p
Peace…

This deep, it's not all song but sometimes
it's all a sham;
I'm not just saying that.
This deep, it's not
all song but sometimes
we repeat ourselves
for clarity.

I'm saying
    walk, stay cautious,
    hands in your pockets where they're safe,
    cigarettes snug in those inter-finger sockets.

I'm saying
    don't cross.

Safety Card Translation, Emergency Exit A

1

Shake, shake
stiff, sweat and look!
dash sightline,
stand still
and distance—
wrench, red and white
exit,
segregate,
square,
still.

2

Falcon side, keen eye
focus!
semi-circle up
around crescent down—
read motion,
turning,
context stance
sideline
wide yellow,
visualize
opening.

3

Contortion
slick metal twist
round redistribution
dancing
and waffle-wobble,
crimped cut club circle,
direction to back-
flip.

4

Red elevation,
yellow lip—wilted sun
furniture,
floor to the
open
attentive
tie-up,
pen to the
draw up
coloured
leverage.

5

Parabola float open
leg and leg up
hand clutch
bedspread slide,
grey left and grey right—
one-foot follow
and try flying, tie-flying,
singular-sky-
directionless rising,
and a ring—endnote: no—
    no attention, no dimension-
    ality no brown no white,
            bubble-black border.

6

Seagull friction,
arms in arms,
yellow,
corner-gripped balloon television
help-pose bicolour flag abstract
layover,
envelope,
    thinning footnote: shadowfloat
    banana, floorstem—
    no lengthened bulb,
    no human figure.

Poem the Moment After

In a drama another image appears
and the rays whiten, something insidious
fanning, rustling unjust against
the surface of the written-off quotidian,
off-ridden,
its depth off
any scale in a gradient
—so far off
you might give way
to the noise hatching: the flood
of the after, the seeping in of joy
so steep it seems a fake.
Too far gone
for fantasy,
it's done.
Like a sound effect
it's done,
that drama a grim, gasping
sticking, peeling, calloused,
sicced.

Humble

Did you catch the ending?
Sure was ecstatic.
I was absorbed

(my skin fissured promptly).
Like a dot / mouth cupping.
From a person, I stood up

(but the *world* knows that).
Adoration of the orange rind.
Roundness of the face

(predisposed to sketching).
I don't know the divided.
I gave the remainder

(to you? or to seeming?).
No claims about questions.
Whatever says, goes

(but consider this nothing).

Interbella:

two little songs

Not One

I saw a pregnant woman on the bus
collect a blonde-haired, red-tied ponytail.
I read a sign that advertised a sale

for men's suits, catching troughs of sun glow
in its gloss and spitting it back out
into the sky. I watched a music video
that sang: seventy million people

do this, do that, keeping the number hallowed,
the notes shivering with the strength of the sum
of all those unique humans, differences swallowed
together. The best numbers are not one,

though you say we have that many minds and souls.
I'd dissolve if I argued, guarding thoughts
like zebra mussels or flocks of white seagulls.

Words for Rain

To put it bluntly, the rain ricocheted
so hard off the 7–eleven sign
that it burned, and the pinprick blankets swayed
like drain water, roving strike-through lines

on straight streets' soaked concrete. In elegant
terms: We were inside, it thunderstormed. Or:
The black clouds loomed, ballooned, till we were ants.
There might be millions more

descriptors; still, the rain remains some billions of drops
across and high.
Mutatis mutandis, it will not stop
resounding, even when I pry

against the ingrown thought with this ripe plum
that coats the wet road purple as the rain hums.

Players

I've Started Waking Up Earlier

One summer I spent every night
awake and wandering. Watched the cartoon
channel that flowed all hours—decades-old
shows draining sharp seconds. Saw
"One Froggy Evening,"
the Broadway-singing frog's phonograph songs
tearing down a world as fast as Acme Construction.
I held my thin, black sleeve
to the lamp. The light shone straight and strong
through every fibre,
emblazoned an asteroid cloud of cotton dust
on my clothes.
                The mornings, now, are like smoke,
even though I'm cleaner and more alert.
I eat breakfast now. I might be nostalgic
if I knew what it meant, but the word won't form
in high numbered hours.
No shade of regret floats like bacteria,
though there is regret.
I solved the mystery of the dark thump
at my door each night near 5 AM.
Sometimes I read the paper.

Picasso's Drawing of Don Quixote and Sancho Panza

The sun is most important
The sun makes everything black as ink
and bakes in the whole depth of the sky

The sun stokes the juice of life in the dull ass
and parches the thin bones of Roccinante
and grows the grass

The sun appears as—what?
As blotches, as blindness,
symbol for the centre of the black cosmos

The sun makes the world of the daytime, too, a dream
The sun symbolizes chivalry
The sun is in the windmill blades' gleam

The sun is in the wind, too, I think,
though I'll need to find out for sure
Unless you trust the sun
Then you don't need to know anything
and the Earth will be already found

After Chance

He rolls up 6 cuts on the die's face, he's
killing it,

6-lettered C H A N C E makes that 6 dance so
devilish

none shall abolish his throwing you
in pigeon-

toed, with two left feet, wearing too-small
ballet shoes

missing a sole and both toes but Oh!
Chance

chains a smoke to those hot coals.
Consider:

If luck's strike lands slow satisfaction
half-ashed,

the other half's crashed, boot to blue screen,
no manual;

other half's crashed 'cause it can't
shift a manual;

other half's crashed on Advil,
and it's asking:

if good judgement's sober, then who's smashed
the gavel?

If what's good's good, then what's good
evil?

Whose wordplay (like *Scrabble*) gets tagged
unbelievable

slang like a face-slap or smack
to the veins

after cherry pops, ovum drops, facts of life
batched up

in baskets and bunny hops, after that cracked
after mass?

And asking
who in their right mind could ask that,

if not for Our Lord Chance,
the rapper?

Distracted

Another element in my cookware
keeps on smacking of death. Well,
depth. The flow scooped it.
Further—a topping was admired by peers but disdained
in terms of honey drip.
It hits me like a wide triangle's vertex:
early days gain the statistics I nightmare,
shut, and swallow, infected i.e. invested
i.e. well dressed. The loud sum
garners me happy as a pocket,
enterprises its potential in a point system.
If you mine for carnage, have no expectation
of slow motion: the forces of artifice
meet you in duels you won't regret.
On the other hand, my intelligence
maintains steadfast privacy. There are three peaks
abducting lineation. Try to retrace your steps.

Studies in Environmentality

FIGURE STUDY: ROWERS READING SERIES

Broadplane topward,
crosses rolling,
stress, juncture, juncture
(dactylic), bob-tilt,
triangle exhale blowhorn,
sleeptalk forward
swerve or
slur, crick,
dissect,
extant buildup
flick & static cutout
shift. Oil, small wheel,
shiny slide,
big contort
lurch soil.

Tuning in to Erin Mouré and a billowing blot and a trick.
Tuning in to flying saucer stains' *pang*; *pain*.
Tuning in to a bop scrap, a hip hop tune,
        a bop scrap and a blast fuzz fuzz.

FIGURE STUDY: BACKYARD AT NIGHT

Bologna limpness
in nudge-twists, sugarcubes
sailing smooth pits
& vast vegetable
bumbles
—excursion—
so spacious,
oh treat this in earnest
its fluid peace
suicide
wishful, block puppeted,
branch spindle
manpower, waddle.

Tuning in to the lighter strike.
Tuning in to the banter of the far balcony party in the night.

FIGURE STUDY: FUNERAL

Three quarters longlegs,
pure schematic upshot,
not tooth-head—uproot,
slivers, emanating. Drink midriff,
a metal spoon stemless
yet pressing, edge-letting
small grains' signals
in.

> *All personnel, please vacate the head.*
> *All personnel, please vacate the head.*
> *The mechanism will continue to operate in your stead.*

Wormhole substance,
air-crisp hilarity
swarming, rub
flatnesses,
sheet plastic jagged.

Tuning in to the interrogating *r*, rustling grass.
Tuning in to sky bulldoze whine and rushing.
Tuning in to mix-up rushing.
Shuffling and rustling.

Advice from My Exes

1

Make quicker exits,
or better yet, don't come around
in the first place;
speak more often, and with less
substance—that is,
messily; make mistakes; never tell
your greatest strength;

it might, like this cliché, weaken you,
or simply flee;
stake claim to every hardship;
treat yourself
like thin enamel; drink often; do not
touch; be afraid
of drowning, and of burning up.

2

Take me deeper
through the rose-folds of your brain,
and keep me;
remember my grooved patterns on your back
when you're washing;
seed where it'll rain; let swell
your swell head;

you should reap the late, last springs;
never pretend
unless you need to, and keep track
of where it leads;
above all, worship something; invest it
in excitement;
don't ever let it out of your sight.

3

Be more ugly;
stop arriving on time; stop taking
the right lanes;
forget things that seem easy,
or, at least, fall
out of practice; allow your stench to ripen
like wet clay;

it might help to remind you, someday,
you're welcome;
know that many people
never climax
and brag coarsely; know
your beauty's limit,
intimately; act stuck up about it.

4

Don't say anything
in the sole interest of safety;
don't say anything
without a taste of pain,
but make exceptions;
don't hesitate to see your open doors
slammed hard;

you should leave some things to burn
behind you;
please, believe in some other misery;
identify, then exaggerate
your enemies; attack what you do not
desire; only desire
so long as it keeps you company.

Love Song for Kazoo

Those uppermost goodnight
balances,
seriously.

One or more shy
and I love you's
help.

Look at us: one,
the other one,
the contrast.

Bubblegum lover,
do you hear these
truth fruits?

Playlist awakenings
fasten
to me.

Your kiss-laden linen's
awash
with emulsion.

Four nostrils spot on
the palette
trapezial.

Almond, half almond,
parentheses,
balaclava.

Tell me, is your
coral bottom
unspun?

Balances, lover,
like a
jelly bean.

I love you. Pause
and call me
favourite.

I Go to See Them Perform Surgery on My Daughter

When the gallery door slid open and people entered,
there was a glancing point. This was lean, a little nervous.
The assistant in the long interval of her unawareness
falling forever, the way a room seems to slide.

To feel the body, I'd driven there and looked.
In one discussion or another, anywhere and still,
the surgeon seemed to be adjusting suffixed forms,
footnotes like nested snakes.

One of the people he had helped care for
had just died of multiple something, and something became
morally degraded about my presence in the room.
But I didn't feel guilty.

"Good, bad, whatever," he said.
The assistant said, "I hate violence."

I watched, but out of some ancient war—
clapper, armourer—what did I do?
Walking down those long and mostly empty streets
as normal as people could be,

one watching the other watch the other,
you see the lies in your excitement. When it was done,
I eased the door open and stood there, waiting for the dark
to soften to the point where I'd left it.

The fact that she was missing. Missing people
never make sense, but what makes sense?
Mass, a tentative attempt, a literal taste
opened by the density of thinking back into it.

***

A few words, a constricted whisper:
He raises his hand to his forehead
and sees himself by the white sun in far peaks.
Man on his back. He was still waiting for her,
and the lover to talk to the sheriff and the wife.
He was still waiting for her; he watched the sister
where she'd met him. He was still waiting for her.
She probably wouldn't know who was going up the stairs
to the bedroom, where Mother lies long dead.

Vertigo

Is it only now
a shape?
Call it "wandering,"
a word
for praying to articulate.
Or call it by its most deserving
nothing, allowing its linking
with the air,
white tower verticality,
from half knot, through the head,
and in the hair.
Up,
a picture,
a present
that opens
into ending, angles, footing,
preservations ticking
lengths of distance,
(suite of strings)
a beading. Fact
that you're already
falling.

Three Night Buses

41 KEELE

Riding it's like bare-handing
steel poles. Like pulling
a skateboard rail grind in a videogame—
single trick, no combo. Cold sound
of rollers. The world resolved
in swift sequence—one,
then another, then another
floodlight over a strip mall.
The world going back.

319 WILSON

The seats on this one are more clearly
red felt. The aisle is not clean,
but people sweep it
for anything valuable, and everyone
takes their transfers with them.
Guys too cool to drive cars are watching
route highlights: neighbouring guns
and guns and ammo shops' iron-shuttered
fronts, the 24-hour
grocery store, the church
of universal love.
Based on the length of its south section's
entrails, you can't take Dufferin north
except by subway,
but the subway's closed.

When we see each other again,
guys—you seem like a bunch
of really cool guys—
when we see each other again
we're doing a whole lot of acid.
Sometimes I just get lost
in my own thoughts, in my own world
when I boot up *Fallout 3*.
I think we can still keep a beat
with Bobby's tom, if we keep going. Guys,
someone's talking
about punching another guy
in the face, and I have to ask
your name, but doesn't everyone talking together
sound like music?

Epistemologies

STOP SIGN

Propose you clutch a thrill;
                    exceed it.
Grey to black magic,
            blacken
    to the spitting embers
                    of a phoenix.
Hear this lipstick twitch
    & scarlet heel—
    it says
                a luckless homonym of your action's
            tense.
                    Red.

Pull over; sirens & distress
& camera's eye reveals it
    octagonally, 3-D glasses'
                criminally
spectacular
                ontology.
    It ribbons a rash,
copper-crooning,

                    & now I'm angry.
            Blood sunset, grapefruit ruby,
turn on the light.
                    Drag your ass
to the district.
    Buy me drinks.

ICE CUBE

Line-draw fishes from the sea
    & drown the breeze;
surrender this particular wave
    to straightening—the colour water
is not & not
        the shade of sky.
Truly energy, it's in flame
    awake & appearing, but it sings best
about sleep.
    Time loops. In song, it's
        a hue that ain't gonna love you,

a black & white movie
    kind of tune. A flaccid banner
        to harmony, that's blue
as neon-azure Kool-
Aid, or losing a day
        of blueberries
    to a belly.

Unlike the mind's every icy likeness,
    unlike any H_2 molecule (they're colourless),
it's royalty you must allow
        to rule you.

HIGHLIGHTER

Think of a stain on white cloth
  & think of the stained state
    of your papers desiccated
  in attics, the wash
     of old things,
  & you will not
    understand the sunshine of yellow,

which is the truer tint in a sky's
    sky blue, wildflowers'
   primer, & ingredient of green.
Retake the light
    from rose & amber; get
  (consider)
yellow:

     blank flavour,
   warm draw, cool edge, heat
   waylaid, electrical marker, light-
ning.
  Caution
  is bright. Indispensability
   is jaundiced &
the pinprick force piercing the galaxy
  is a coward.

For MF DOOM

THE NAME'S DOOM, AND IT WILL BE REPEATED
UNTIL THE COSMOS BOW DOWN, AND HIS FLOW
RAINBOWS OVER ALL THE VEGETABLE GARDENS
IN BROOKLYN. FACE SOUNDING LIKE AN OBOE,

UNSUNG MASK, FINGERS CLACK-TAPPING, DIE-CAST,
THE MAN HATH WALKED THE BLAST-PATH OF GOD
WITH A HERO'S BEADY EYES SEWN IN BEHIND
HIS PANTYHOSE.

                        WHO YOU CALLIN' ODD?

WHO YOU CALLIN' JUST BEFORE LIGHTS OUT,
BE THEY JAIL-CELL, KNOCKOUT, OR SOL? NOBODY
COMEBACKS EVERY TIME, AND THAT'S WHY DOOM
ALWAYS SCREWS UP HIS LYRICS SO NUTTY,

STRAIGHT TO THE MARTYRDOM OF GROOVE, WHILE LIFE
PLAYS THE INSTRUMENT YOU'VE NEVER HEARD OF.

Connections

You've recently dyed your hair;
on Tuesday at work
you had black hair, freckles,
and sat down right in front of me.

We took turns sneaking glances
at each other. We braced
ourselves and you gave me a smile,
paused, continued walking.

I've seen you a handful of times since
June, always downtown.

We waited for the streetcar
at Spadina and Queen last night
around past midnight.
You sat near the door.

I was wearing a black hat
and overcoat. You—
redhead, glasses, skinny jeans…
got off at Bloor subway.

I always sit across from you,
I'm not sure you've noticed.

We rode together on the bus today.
We glanced at each other
and got on. You were wearing a beige
knit zip up sweater

and carrying a blue foam mat.
We both got off at St. George
station, and as we were climbing up
the stairs you slightly touched

my hand. We looked at each other
briefly. I liked your smile.

Lush

I just thought of something terrible but I'm going to say it anyway.
Pork-barrelling with you,
I admit this feels like it's a summer.

Lush, lucky, *lupis*.
Because the critique is susceptible to the critique,
they have been looking for a staff writer for over a year.

Pointless, anyway.
Sheep, clay, wood and wheat, locked up and in the bank
and brought up out of a hole by your unsoberness.

What will be there when you turn over another rock?
Try our delicious new item.
With these sturdy shoes, I promise I'll be unstoppable.

Goodbye

1

—we vocalize a closing
like a garage door,
or the warm, great wing
of a bird, & the word
clamours like a folding chair,
hard-backed & fast
& soon stacked

2

—lacking good heart,
the good-heartedness in the shape
of a gutted fish the self
takes,
stale air
in the ego,
emptiest type of waste

3

—not the sense,
not the sound, not the scent,
but the drop of the dropped copper
coin, the dust blown
from ground; the whole character
of descent, fair attempt
& failure

Or

—an attempt at failure, safe
in the belly-boiled sounds' centres dampened
in goodbye, the old word
richly hallowed, a hollow object
& halo, an open ring
& crown atop the timeline;

it's what might have been, had we not
already been saying goodbye.

Addenda:
two essays

On a Broken Gif

http://0.media.collegehumor.cvcdn.com/51/69/9fc1f4a928590f1420256
6a5d7749b27-gif-glitch-14.gif

What's most unravelling is the reset from the descent to the all-normal:
    normal scene, normal person, normal meme.
The colour balance seems to morph, mathematically, back and forth,
    in this orbit of brokenness,
and impresses the indifferent role of cold code in *weird*—that is, fate,
    the inevitable uncanny.

Along a thread, a fibrous simultaneity, interweaving of headless carnival
    and fixed digital linearity,
remember: whether or not we perceive, distinctly, two qualities in
    this scene is irrelevant.
How is it that we read?

Unlacing several concept-spaces, needlepoint severing rhizome logics
    therefore incommensurable, perfectly boundaried.
But pointing is a means of being—being pointing material, being
    meaningful, being a malleable realing.
My design is to point and the point pervades me, constitutively invades
    me, shares my anatomy with any other pointing being.

No gesture's unidirectional. We're drawing a light play: one finger
    forward and a hand curling back three,
how a crab walks lateral. The line is flat, hard and alive.
To define its end with illusive necessity, directing and heavying, is
    enlightening—the pointing being material, pointing meaning.

Enlightenment, then, is the creation of revelation, immaculate birth
        of surface and depth and their ingrown derivative, seeing,
genetically into the world and as *things*,
writing a lighting out for the Territory.
Pointing material becomes a name for anything. Name another.

On the Ground

If my sole is sutured to the concrete by something that won't give up,
    let's count that a pole to aspire to: absolute self-centredness *qua*
        stubbornness *qua* force.
What's tough is cutting up the crowd, charting out the organs—
    balancing our apple on the individual.

This should be everywhere out there: *one* name, *one* gravitation, *one*
    suture, *one* force,
one undividable *in* dividuals, contextualized and thus confided, thus
    divided. *Why?*
already ruins it—*for what causality?* lies between (more than one) things,
lies there with intention, in a direction, in tension against me, I, myself.
(Keep in mind how we split up every time we use a compound.)

Now *what?*—imperatively: *explain <u>the presence</u> of this thing*—that's
    the *one*:
describe at once <u>the thing</u> as everything (excluding every thing), or *what's*
<u>the one missing</u> from the one I spoke? Like a wheelbarrow,
all is not to be thought at one go.
Hear, I speak one real word for ground: _____

Notes

"To KiD CuDi": The poem responds primarily to KiD CuDi's "Pursuit of Happiness."

"How to Hustle": The epigraph is from Jay Z's "U Don't Know."

"Drunken Master": The title refers to the 1994 Jackie Chan film *Drunken Master II*, also titled *The Legend of Drunken Master*.

"Myself as a Dictator": The poem is written entirely with vocabulary taken from Hannah Arendt's *The Origins of Totalitarianism*.

"Future Statement": The poem is an ekphrastic response to Andrew Duff's *Quasi-spin* (2014), and other paintings.

"TV's Jon Dore on Jon Dore and *The Jon Dore Television Show*": The poem is based on the Comedy Network television series that ran from 2007 to 2009, and its eponymous star.

"Safety Card Translation, Emergency Exit A": The poem's six sections translate the six panels of the exit procedure for emergency exit A depicted on WestJet's Boeing 737-600/700 safety card.

"Not One": The video alluded to is the music video for "70 Million" by Hold Your Horses.

"After Chance": Many of the poem's phrases, images, and puns are taken, with modifications, from various recordings by Chance the Rapper.

"I Go to See Them Perform Surgery on My Daughter": Nearly all of the poem's lines are taken from Don DeLillo's *Point Omega* (Scribner, 2010). The poem was composed by combining sentence fragments from the ends and beginnings of the novel's pages, in order, but skipping pages in between.

"Connections": All of the poem's phrases are taken from posts on craigslist Toronto's missed connections section.

"On a Broken Gif": The second to last line is taken from "Chapter the Last" of Mark Twain's *Adventures of Huckleberry Finn.*

"On the Ground": The second to last line is taken from Jacques Derrida's *Of Grammatology* (Trans. Gayatri Spivak).

"Desk Index" is an alphabetized list of every occurrence of every textual phrase printed or inscribed on an item on or in my bedroom desk on the date of collection, August 6, 2013.

Acknowledgements

Many thanks, first of all, to David Bateman, without whose encouragement I may never have endeavoured to produce a manuscript.

Many thanks to all those who read and offered their thoughts on previous versions of the collection, especially Miles Forrester, Naomi Freeman, David Hickey, Rasiqra Revulva, and Derek Shank. Special thanks to Jim Johnstone, who edited the manuscript for print; I am deeply grateful for your perspective, support, and friendship. Many thanks also to the team at Palimpsest Press for their noble efforts, and for making me feel at home.

Many thanks to the organizers of reading series and events at which I've performed; without your work, we are all lost. Special thanks to Edward Nixon, for keeping me on my toes, and to Stan Burfield.

Many thanks to my creative writing instructors at York University and Vanderbilt University, especially Michael Helm, whose generosity and wisdom have kept me writing through the years.

Many thanks to all of those writers and thinkers with whom I've had the privilege of participating in writing workshops; you will always be my first and best readers. Special thanks to Emily Pohl-Weary and all of the Parkdale/Toronto Street Writers; without you, I would not be what I am. Special thanks to Devin P. L. Edwards, Sarah Varnam, Miles Forrester, and Kevin Heslop, in friendship. Special thanks to Amanda Boulos, for the limitless gifts of conversation and distraction.

Many thanks to my family and friends for their continuing support and enthusiasm.

Finally, many thanks to all those I've forgotten; your omission, I promise, is by necessity and not by choice.

Earlier versions of several of these poems have previously appeared in online and print publications, all of which I'd like to acknowledge for their support and dedication:

"Connections," "Exit," "Three Night Buses," and "Words for Rain" first appeared in *Sewer Lid* 1 in February 2016. "Naked Baby" first appeared in *(parenthetical)* 10 in November 2015. "Goodbye" first appeared in *Futures Trading* 3.3 in November 2015. "Nosferatu" first appeared in *The Quilliad* 6 in October 2015; "When You Need Water" first appeared in issue 2 in October 2013; "Not One" first appeared in the magazine's debut issue in June 2013. "Lush" first appeared in *text* 3 in March 2015. "Bouquet" and "Picasso's Drawing of Don Quixote and Sancho Panza" first appeared in *Hamilton Arts and Letters* 6.2 in December 2013. "Bibliophile" and "Epistemologies" both appeared online in *ditch* in July 2013. "I've Started Waking Up Earlier" first appeared in *Cordite Poetry Review* 42 in June 2013. "The Mole Rat" first appeared on the League of Canadian Poets' National Poetry Month blog in April 2013.

"Desk Index" has been published in multiple chapbook editions by the author in 2013 and 2014. "How to Hustle," "Humble" and "Studies in Environmentality" first appeared in *an erratic sample* (2014), a limited edition chapbook by the author, along with reprints of "Bouquet," "Bibliophile," "Epistemologies" and "When You Need Water."

Desk Index

40, 40
40W, 40W, 40W, 40W, 40W, 40W
4418A-CU0006, 4418A-MR0020
5, 5, 5, 5, 5, 5, 5, 5, 5, 5, 5, 5, 5
50500mA
53148
540U
5416
55mA
5B2F2350
5RD00F2
5V, 5V
6, 6, 6, 6, 6, 6, 6, 6, 6, 6, 6, 6
60
60930-1
60950-1
60Hz, 60Hz, 60Hz, 60Hz
620AL
6235ANHMW, 6235ANHMW
649E-6235ANH
'69
7, 7, 7, 7, 7, 7, 7, 7, 7
70
72716
8, 8, 8, 8, 8, 8, 8, 8
80
80C
8124
820-003408
82803
8GB
8K89
9, 9, 9, 9, 9, 9
90
9V, 9V

A, A, A, A, A, a, a, a
A3L6235ANH
A/a
above
AC, AC
Accessory
AC-DC
ACRILICA
ACROLEN-GRUNDIERUNG
ACRYLIC
ACRYLIQUE
actiion
ADAPTOR
adhering
admission
Admittance
Agencia
ALL, all, all
ALLE
Alt, Alt
ALUMNI, ALUMNI
AMPLIFIED
ANATEL
and, and, and, and, and, and, and, and
ANSI/UL
anti
any
Appliance
Approval, Approval
April
AR
Arden
are, are, are, are, are
ARTIST, ARTIST, ARTIST
ARTISTAS

ARTISTE
As
ASAP, ASAP
Assembled
at
ATTENTION-RISQUE
AWM, AWM

B, B, B, B, B, B
BA68-06426A, BA68-08894A
Backspace
BASS
be
Bee
behaviour
Bentonville
BIC, BIC, BIC
BLOOR, BLOOR, BLOOR, BLOOR,
    BLOOR, BLOOR, BLOOR, BLOOR,
    BLOOR, BLOOR, BLOOR, BLOOR,
    BLOOR, BLOOR, BLOOR, BLOOR,
    BLOOR, BLOOR, BLOOR, BLOOR,
    BLOOR, BLOOR, BLOOR, BLOOR,
    BLOOR, BLOOR, BLOOR, BLOOR,
    BLOOR, BLOOR, BLOOR, Bloor
Brock
BT, BT, Bt
By, by, by

C, C, C, C, C, C
C-10459
C22.2, C22.2
C30
C-8942
C-9015
C.A., CA-101D

CALIDAD
cameras
CANADA, Canada, Canada
CANVAS, CANVAS, CANVAS
CAPA
Caps
capture
CAUIDADO-RIESGO
cause
CAUTION-RISK
CCA109LP0450T1
CCAH12LP0170T0
CCAMOLP0500T2
CE, CE, CE, CE, CE, CE
certain
CERTIFIED
CFL, CFL, CFL
change
CHARGER
CHINA, CHINA, CHINA, China,
    China, China, China, China, China,
China/Fabricado
Chine
CHOIX
CINEMA, CINEMA, CINEMA,
    CINEMA, CINEMA, CINEMA,
    CINEMA, CINEMA, CINEMA,
    CINEMA, CINEMA, CINEMA,
    CINEMA, CINEMA, CINEMA,
    CINEMA, CINEMA, CINEMA,
    CINEMA, CINEMA, CINEMA,
    CINEMA, CINEMA, CINEMA,
    CINEMA, CINEMA, CINEMA,
    CINEMA, CINEMA, CINEMA,
    CINEMA, Cinema, cinema, cinema,
    cinema, cinema, cinema's

Class, Class
Classe
CLASSMAT
Club
CM
CMIIT, CMIIT
CNC, CNC, CNC
Co., Co.
COBY, Coby
CODE
COLORANTES
Complies, Complies, Complies, Comply
CONDITIONÉE
CONFORMS
Contains
Contiene
CORE
Corp.
courtesy
CSA, CSA
Ctrl, Ctrl
C-U0006

D, D, D
D2L-M-R0020, D2L-C-U0006
D3027
D8101104
DB
DB101104
DC, DC
DCC
DE, DE, DE, DE, de, de, de, de
Début
Del
Delete

Deli
Desktop
devices, devices
DIPLÔMÉS, DIPLÔMÉS
discretion
DIXON
DOBLE
DOCS, DOCS, DOCS, DOCS, DOCS,
DOCS, DOCS, DOCS, DOCS,
DOCS, DOCS, DOCS, DOCS,
DOCS, DOCS, DOCS, DOCS,
DOCS, DOCS, DOCS, DOCS,
DOCS, DOCS, DOCS, DOCS,
DOCS, DOCS, DOCS, Docs
DODGE
Dongshun
DOUBLE, DOUBLE, DOUBLE
DQA-2049
Drive
during

E, E, E, E, E, E, E
E149716FC
E321011, E321011
Échap
Electric, Electrical
electronic, Electronics, Electronics
EMPLOYEZ
EN, EN, en, en, en
End
ENERGY, energy
engaging
Enter, entering
ENTRADA
entry, entry
ENUMEREES

INPUT, INPUT, Input
Insert/Inser
inside, inside, inside
Inspired
Intel, Intel, Intel, Intel
International
INTERTEK
is
I.T.E., I.T.E.

J, J
JNZCU0006
JNZMR0020
journal
Jun

K, K
KCC-CRM-INT-6235ANHMW
KÜNSTLER-LEINWÄNDE

L, L, L, L
Late
Leadfast
LED
LEFT
LIENZO
LISTED, LISTED, LISTED, LISTED,
    Listed
LITTLEBURGUNDYSHOES.COM
Lock, Lock
Logitech, Logitech
London
LOS
Ltd., Ltd.
LYONS, LYONS, Lyons
LZ207AH

M, M, M, M, m
M210
MADE, MADE, Made, Made, Made,
    Made, Made, Made, Made, Made,
maj.
Management, management's
Marca
Marketed, marketing
materials
Mattel
MAX, MAX, MAX, MAX, MAX,
    MAX, MAX, MAX
MDR-E818
ME06
media
MEDIEN
MEDIOS
MEDIUMS
memberships
Memory
miel
M/N, M/N
MODEL, MODEL, Model, Model,
MODELO, Modelo
módulo
MONTADO
MP620-8G
M-R0020
MULTIMEDIA
must

N, N, N, N
N176
N231
N31
N363

NA4LBHZT
Nacional
Nemko
NEXXTECH, NEXXTECH
NMB-003
No, No., No., No., no, no
No.12
NOKIA, NOKIA
NOM
NORMAL
not
note
NOTEBOOK
NP540U3C, NP540U3C-ADICA
N-TICKET
NYCE

O, O, O, O
O69
objectionable
OF, of, of of, of
off
OFF/DIRECT
older
on, on
ON/AMP
Only
operators
OR, or, or, or, or, or
ORIOLE
otherwise
ots
OU
owners

P, P, P
PANEL
paper, paper, paper
PAR
PARA, PARA
Patrons
PD96235ANH
PEINTRE, PEINTRES
permitted, permitting
PgDn/P.suiv.
PgUp/P.préc.
PHONE
photographs
Picture
PID
Please, please
PM
P/N, P/N
policies
portions
Pots
POUR, POUR
POWER, POWER
PREMIER
PREMIUM
present
PRIMERA
PRIMED
Product, Product
Program
promotional
Prt

Q, Q

that
THE, THE, THE, THE, THE, THE,
   THE, THE, THE, THE, THE,
   THE, THE, THE, THE, THE,
   THE, THE, THE, the, the, the, the,
   the, the, the, the, the
their
theory
There
those
threshold
ticket, ticket, ticketholders, tickets
times
TIPO
TM
TO, TO, TO, TO, TO, to, to, to, to, to,
   to, to
TODOS
TOILE
TOUTES
turn
TYPE, TYPE, Type

U, U, U, U, U
UCI
UL, UL, UL, UL, UL, UL-60950-1
ULTRA
Ultrabook
UNIVERSITÉ
UNIVERSITY
unless
unused, unused
upping
US, US, US, US
U.S.A.

USE, USE, USE, use

V, V
V2.0
Verr.
video, video
VOLUME
VW-1, VW-1

W, W, W
Walmart, Walmart.com
Warranty
WELCOME
WERTVOLLE
Western
which
WI
Wifi
will
WIND
with, with, with, with, with, with
WLAN
WW
WWW
www.clarknovabooks.com,
   www.clarknovabooks.com,
   www.clarknovabooks.com,
   www.clarknovabooks.com,
   www.clarknovabooks.com,
   www.clarknovabooks.com

X, X

Y, Y
years

YORK, YORK, YORK
YOU, you
YOUR, your

Z, Z
Z1284
Z855
Zhejiang
ZWEIFACHE

John Nyman's verse, visual, and conceptual poems and poetics have appeared in a variety of print and online publications including *Rampike*, (*parenthetical*), *Cordite Poetry Review*, and *Hamilton Arts and Letters*. Originally from Toronto, he is currently completing a PhD in Theory and Criticism at Western University in London, Ontario.